Welcome

Enjoy

The Creative

World

Of

D. McDonald

And

Thank

You

For

Purchasing

This

Book!

d.mcdonald designs

Presents:

Branching Out

"Because You are Never Too Old to Color!"

Branching Out

First Edition Printed May 2016
Copyright ©2016
D.McDonald's Branching Out
All Rights Reserved

More of the work of D.McDonald can be found at:

www.facebook.com/DMcDonaldDesigns

Welcome to another D.McDonald Collection
Of coloring pages designed for adults which can also
be a magical journey for children as well and even
more so when colored with an adult!

In this collection you will see that one image has
been placed so it has a frame and followed by the
larger unframed design. It is nice to have choices!
Please be sure to place cardstock behind the image you
are coloring because the paper is thin! The plus side to
this is that the design that is created by the bleed is
also interesting and feel free to play with it. Many
people choose to take the book apart and have it printed
on cardstock. You are encouraged to make copies for
your own use and to share with family and friends
(buying them their very own copy is wonderful as
well). At the end of this book are samples of other
coloring collections by D. McDonald of D. McDonald
Designs. Experiment, embellish, and above all else just
simply Enjoy!

Your purchase of this book and other books by D.
McDonald is greatly appreciated and please do make
contact on Facebook and share your colored creations!

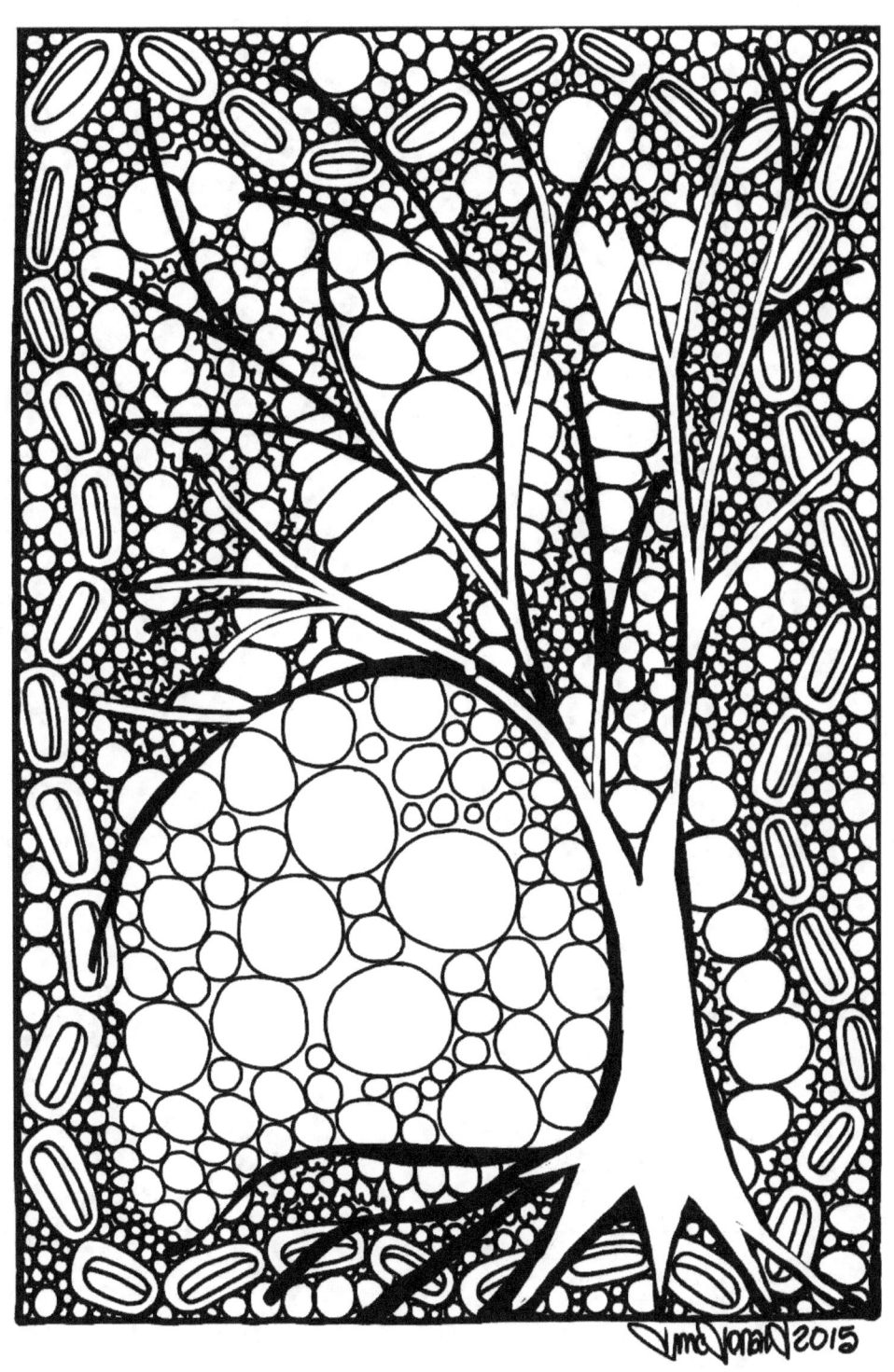

JmcDonald 2015

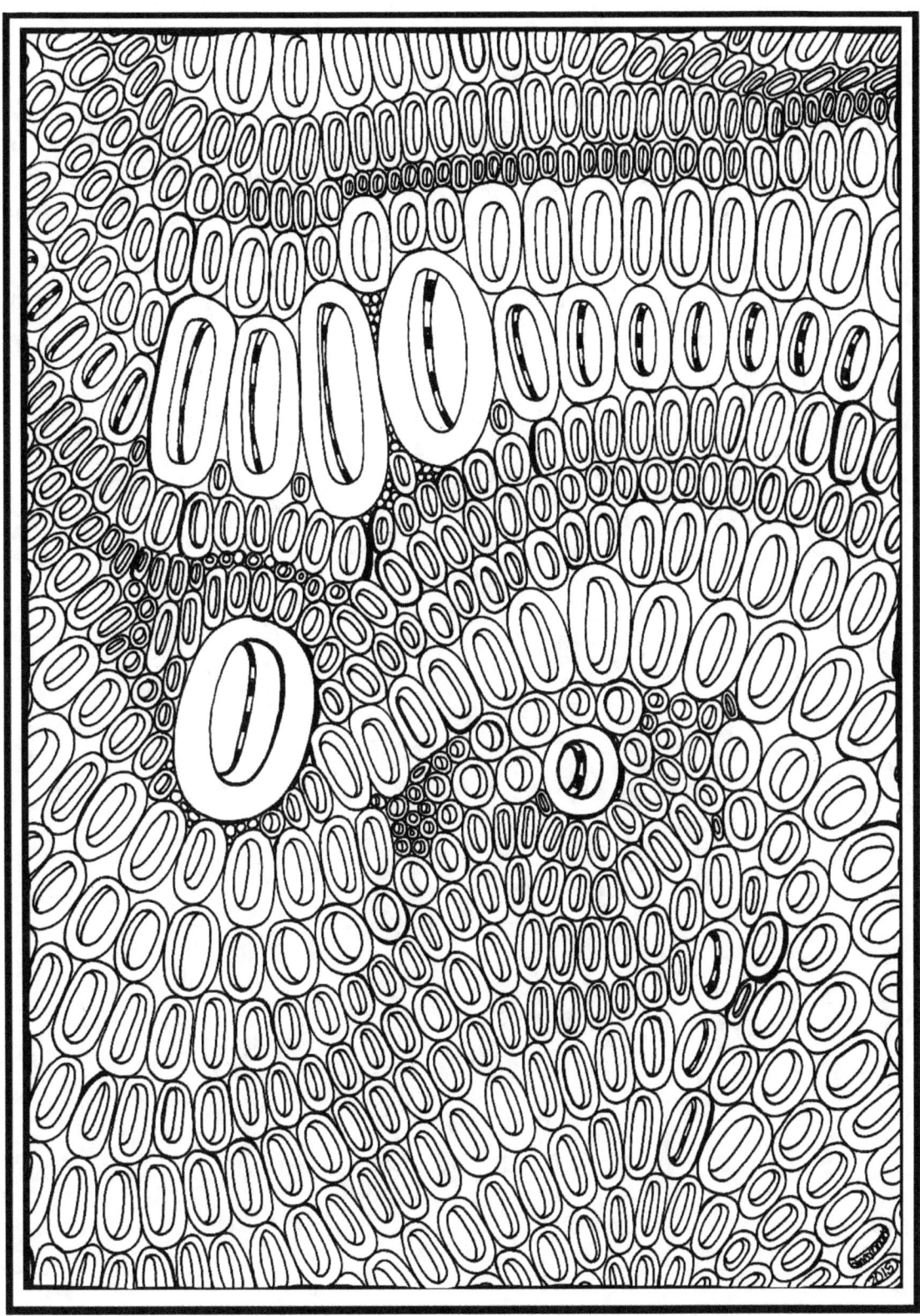

Now Available on Amazon

DMcDonald DeSigns presents:
The Adult Coloring Buffet
a little of this and that
a taste of ~ debness ~
to color and enjoy

40 ILLUSTRATIONS
Printed on single-sided 60 lb. bright white paper.

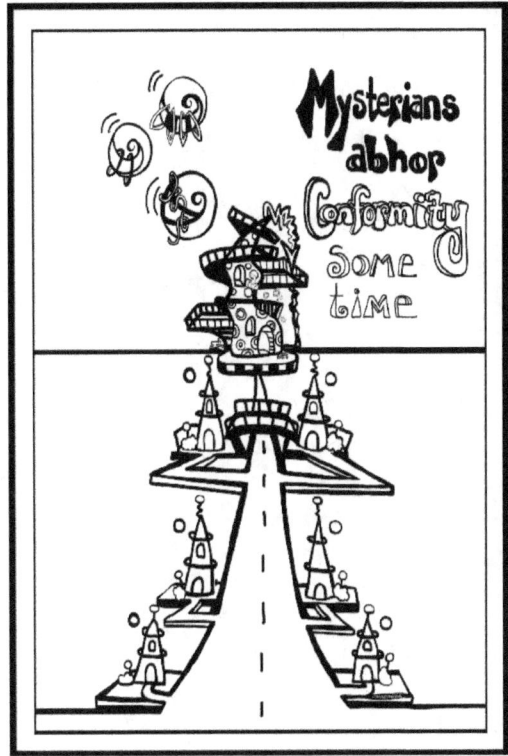

MYSTERIA
DMcDONALD'S
QUIRKY BOOK
TO COLOR
AND READ,
TO PASS ALONG
FOR FUTURE GENERATIONS
ABOUT A PLACE
WHERE EVERYTHING
IS AND IS NOT
WHERE NOTHING MAKES
SENSE
BUT IT DOES !
DMCDONALD'S
MYSTERIA

SAMPLES FROM: d.McDonald Designs Floral Adult Coloring Book Collection

Hope You Had Fun and Relaxed as you colored!